Contents

Published by the Usk Valley Walk Partnership

Dawn Mist at Pant-y-Goitre

Whilst less well known than the Wye Valley the Usk Valley matches it for beauty. From its source on Fan Foel in the Brecon Beacons National Park the river flows through Brecon along a broad valley separating the Brecon Beacons and the Black Mountains. Below Crickhowell it crosses from the county of Powys into Monmouthshire, once part of the ancient kingdom of Gwent. From Abergavenny it meanders past quiet hamlets and villages; the historic market town of Usk; the former Roman fortress of Isca, now Caerleon, entering the Severn Estuary at Newport.

The River Usk escaped the ravages of the Industrial Revolution that for so long blighted the other rivers of the South Wales Valleys, thus retaining its natural course and its importance as a salmon river.

For most of the year the Usk is benign with its tumbling, fast flowing waters being separated by long, deep, quiet pools. At times of heavy rains, however, its character can suddenly and dramatically change. Each winter the Usk threatens to engulf the towns and villages along its banks.

The Kingdom of Gwent has down the ages been of strategic importance to the successive waves of invaders seeking to control the borders between the lowland and highland areas of South Wales. The Usk Valley forges a natural route into the Brecon Beacons, the Black Mountains and the interior uplands, its turbulent history attesting to how frequently this area has been disputed. Some of the strongholds of the Celts, the Romans, the Normans, the Marcher Lords and the Welsh Princes are seen along the route.

Small ironworks had been established in this south-eastern corner of Wales as early as the mid 16th century. The easily accessible iron ore, limestone, ample supplies of timber for charcoal and fast flowing streams for power, providing an ideal location for the development of the industry. Later, the presence of large reserves of coal began an iron-making boom, which was to change the face of this part of Wales. Throughout the walk you will come across evidence of the impact of this early industrialisation and nearby sites such as that at the Clydach Gorge, are an industrial archaeologist's paradise.

The former Monmouthshire and Abergavenny Canals were both opened in the late 18th century. In 1812 they were joined to create the Monmouthshire and Brecon canal thus providing a continuous route from Newport to Brecon. The main water supply for the canal was taken from the river Usk via a weir above Brecon. The water left the weir and actually passed right under the town to run into the canal at its terminus.

This waterway conveyed iron ore from the south, and brought vital supplies of limestone and coal to the towns on the upper reaches. Whilst the barges predominantly carried industrial goods, the local farming communities used them to take produce and, sometimes, livestock to the markets. The canal companies also encouraged passenger traffic by publishing timetables.

The coming of the railways in the 1840s saw a steady decline in the commercial importance of this once busy waterway and by the early 1930s trade along the canal had virtually ceased as had any maintenance of the waterway and it was allowed to become derelict.

There are now over 30 miles of navigable water from Brecon in the north to Crown Bridge just below Pontypool, in the south. As the only canal within a National Park, running through a landscape of outstanding beauty, this section of the Usk Valley Walk is very special.

Buckland Old Mill

The Brecon Beacons National Park was established in 1957 under the National Parks and Access to the Countryside Act of 1949. The two statutory purposes of the National Park Authority as defined by the 1995 Environment Act, are to conserve and enhance the natural beauty, wildlife and cultural heritage of the Park and to promote opportunities for the enjoyment and understanding of its special qualities. The Act also gives the Park Authority a duty to seek to foster the economic and social well being of their local communities.

The Park is spread over 520 square miles (1346 sq.km) of spectacular landscape, dominated by a long backbone of mountains and moorlands that descend into valleys with farms and villages dotted amongst the patchwork quilt of small fields and enclosures. Much of the land is in private ownership; some belongs to bodies such as Forest Enterprise, the National Trust and the National Park Authority which owns large areas of common land.

There are three National Park Visitor Centres; the Mountain Centre in Libanus, Craig-y-Nos Country Park and the Danywenallt Study Centre. There are also three Information Centres at Brecon, Llandovery and Abergavenny and ten Village Information Centres dotted about the Park. All of these centres offer detailed information and advice on local walks and amenities in the National Park. Please call 01874 624437 for any further information, visit the Brecon Beacons web site www.breconbeacons.org, or contact them by e-mail: enquiries@breconbeacons.org.

Towards Abergavenny

River Usk near Glangrwyney

The main line of the Monmouthshire and Brecon Canal meanders south from Brecon and is located within the Brecon Beacons National Park for its first 32 miles (51.5 kilometres). It then makes its way for a further 8 miles (13 kilometres) through Pontymoile and Cwmbran to Newport. At Newport it once went as far as Pillgwenlly, but is now truncated at the entrance to Barrack Hill Tunnel 2.5 miles (4 km) from its original terminus.

The upper section of some 34 miles (55 km) from Brecon to the top of Five Locks in Cwmbran is fully navigable and is a popular tourist attraction. Though isolated from the rest of the British canal network it is considered by many as the most picturesque canal in Britain. It supports hire and day boat companies, trip boats and private moorings for which there is a waiting list.

Although at present the 6 miles (9.5 km) at the southern end of the Canal are not navigable these are well used by walkers, cyclists and anglers. Much work has been done in the recent past to preserve this waterway corridor for a broad spectrum of leisure uses.

The Crumlin Arm contains the impressive Fourteen Locks which has been given Ancient Monument status in view of their unique nature. This arm is currently 8 miles long (13 km), being truncated at Cwmcarn some 3 miles (5 km) short of its original destination.

Further details can be obtained from:

British Waterways, Waterway Office, The Wharf, Govilon, Nr Abergavenny NP7 9NY Tel: 01873 830328 Fax: 01873 831788 www.britishwaterways.co.uk. Open Monday - Friday. Provides information on private and weekly/day hire boating, canoeing, fishing, educational resources and events.

British Waterways, Goytre Wharf Heritage, Activity and Study Centre, Goytre Wharf, Llanover, Nr Abergavenny NP7 9EW Tel/Fax: 01873 881069 www.britishwaterways.co.uk. open all year round.

The Centre has something for everyone, from offering the visitor an opportunity to learn more about the canal or just browse in the Art Gallery, to an exhibition of the South Wales Tramroads. Its facilities can provide a base for educational, training and corporate functions, craft demonstrations, workshops and group activities, with the Tea Room offering refreshments to all visitors.

Llangattock Wharf

ORDNANCE SURVEY MAPS

The most useful maps for walkers are those to 1/25000 scale (4cm to 1km or 2 1/2 inches to 1 mile) published by the Ordnance Survey. OS Explorer Map No 152 (Newport and Pontypool) covers the southern part of the walk from Caerleon to Chain Bridge and OS Explorer Map OL 13 (Brecon Beacons National Park Eastern Area) and OL 12 (West and Central areas) cover the route from Chain Bridge to Brecon. The Explorer OL maps are double-sided.

THE ROUTE

The Usk Valley Walk is 48 miles (77 km) long, and runs from Caerleon, near Newport, in the south, to Brecon. The walk never strays very far away from the river and from Llanellen onwards, it utilises part of the towpath of the Monmouthshire and Brecon Canal. The highest point reached is 1,000 ft above sea level: the amount of ascent and descent encountered is limited to a few short, sharp climbs. Significant sections of the walk follow a canal towpath, but level does not mean low. The canal follows the 360 ft contour for much of its length.

The route of the Usk Valley Walk is subject to regular upgrading and improvement. This is the third edition of a walking guide which was first published in 1989. It contains several variations of the route since the previous edition appeared and certain Ordnance Survey maps were published.

The route variations are at:
Llantrisant - OS Explorer Map 152.
Llangynidr and Aber (Talybont) - OS Explorer OL 13

Please note that the Usk Valley Walk is not indicated as a recreational footpath on the Outdoor Leisure Maps. The route is so shown on the Explorer Map, but the route variation is not indicated.

DISTANCES & TIMES

The times given to walk each section assume a moderate walking pace. No allowance is made for stops or sightseeing. The differences in time reflect the difficulty of the walking and the terrain.

WAYMARKS

The walk is marked by markers with the Otter symbol on them, which also appears on the front cover of this guide. The otter symbol was chosen because the River Usk was one of the few rivers in which otters were able to survive the dramatic decline in their habitat.

You will also follow standard path waymarks, usually yellow arrows to indicate footpaths. Blue arrows indicate bridleways and white arrows indicate paths where access has been permitted by a landowner.

PUBLIC RIGHTS OF WAY

Most of the Usk Valley Walk follows public rights of way, but the land they cross is private. Please keep to the line of the path and follow the waymarks where provided. Do not linger longer than necessary or stray from the waymarked route. If the path has to be diverted for any reason, such as the replacement of a footbridge, please follow the waymarks rather than the map until you are guided back to the main route. Where cultivation has occurred the course of the path should have been reinstated and made clear.

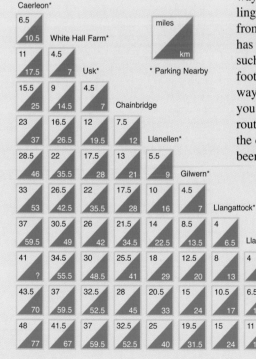

RIGHTS OF WAY AUTHORITIES

In Newport, public rights of way are the responsibility of Countryside Team, Public Protection & Environmental Services, Newport City Council, Newport. NP20 4UR Telephone 01633 244491.

In Monmouthshire, they are the responsibility of the Corporate Director - Environment, County Hall, Cwmbran NP44 2XH Tel 01633 644860 and in the Brecon Beacons National Park they are the responsibility of the National Park Authority.

CAR PARKING

There are car parks/parking spaces close to the walk at Caerleon, White Hall Farm, Usk, Llanellen, Llanfoist, Gilwern, Llangattock, Llangynidr, Aber, Pencelli and Brecon. Please do not leave your car in a pub car park without seeking the landlord's permission first. If you are staying locally it should be possible to leave your car at your accommodation address. Please avoid parking on roadside verges, in field entrances and passing spaces. Don't forget to lock your car and hide or take valuables with you or best of all leave them at home.

LOCAL ACCOMMODATION

There are numerous farmhouses, guesthouses, inns and hotels offering bed and breakfast in the area as well as some self-catering establishments and camp sites. A separate free guide is regularly produced for the Usk Valley Walk. If you did not receive one when you purchased this guide please contact any of the Tourist Information Centres who will be pleased to send it to you free of charge.

INFORMATION CENTRES

For everything you need to know about the Vale of Usk - what to see, where to stay, and how to get there please contact one of the following Tourist Information Centres.

Newport TIC Tel 01633 842962
Fax 01633 222615
Museum & Art Gallery,
John Frost Square
Newport NP9 1HZ

Caerleon TIC Tel/Fax 01633 422656
5 High Street, Caerleon NP6 1AE

Abergavenny TIC Tel 01873 857588
Fax 01873 850217
Swan Meadow, Monmouth Road
Abergavenny NP7 5HH

Brecon Beacons National Park
Information Centre
Tel 01874 623156

*Crickhowell TIC**
Tel 01873 812105
Beaufort Chambers,
Beaufort Street
Crickhowell NP8 1AA
* Denotes seasonal opening*

Brecon TIC Tel 01874 622485
Fax 01874 625256
Cattle Market Car Park
Brecon LD3 9DA

GIANT HOGWEED

This huge plant which is a native of the Caucasus mountains between Russia and Turkey, was introduced to Britain as an ornamental plant in the late 19th century. It is now widespread throughout the British Isles, especially along river banks and it is very common along sections of the Usk Valley Walk.

This perennial plant can grow up to 5 metres tall, with huge leaves up to 1 metre across. Each plant can produce more than 50,000 seeds per year which can remain viable for 15 years.

It should not be touched without wearing protective clothing.
If the sap comes into contact with the skin, in the presence of sunlight, can cause severe irritation, swelling and blistering.

Do not touch Giant Hogweed: seek medical advice if blistering occurs.

SAFE WALKING AND WEATHER

When out walking for several hours please let someone know where you are going and how long you expect to take. Plan your walk ahead, take a map/guide book with you and wear appropriate clothing and stout shoes or boots. Although the terrain is never difficult, the path can be muddy and the undergrowth lush and gaiters/over-trousers may be necessary in all but the driest conditions. A small rucksack for extra clothing, waterproofs and a snack is ideal when walking in inclement weather. In sunny weather be sure to have adequate sun protection and carry a drink to avoid dehydration.

DOGS

Please remember that dogs should follow the line of the path with you and be aware they can cause alarm and distress to farm animals and wildlife, sometimes triggering aggressive behaviour especially if they have young with them. It is an offence to allow a dog to attack or chase livestock and it is advisable always to keep dogs on a lead when walking through sheep enclosures, passing near to livestock and close to farmyards. Please ensure your dog is wormed regularly to prevent livestock infection.

DOGS AND CATTLE
Advice for dog owners

- Be prepared for cattle to react to your presence especially when you have a dog with you.
- Move carefully and quietly and if possible walk around them.
- Remember to close gates behind you.
- Keep your dog under close control and on a short lead.
- Don't hang on to your dog if you are threatened by animals - let it go.
- Don't put yourself at risk. Find another way round and rejoin the footpath as soon as possible.
- Don't get between a cow and her calf.
- Don't panic! Most cows will stop before they reach you. If they follow, just walk on quietly.
- Don't forget to report any problems to the local authority.

WALKERS' QUESTIONNAIRE

The local authorities and other agencies who manage and maintain the Usk Valley Walk welcome your feedback, good and bad! Your comments will help us to make sure we are providing what you, the walker, wants. If you can suggest any improvements to the route, the waymarking or this guide, please let us know, so that we can make things better for those who use the walk in the future. Even if you found everything in good order and the walk was a pleasure, apart from the weather and the odd blister, it would be nice to know that too. When reporting problems, please provide as much information as possible about the location, ideally with a photocopied map or grid reference.

Bluebells, Coed y Bwnydd

COUNTRY COURTESY

Although you may not meet many people on the walk, remember the countryside is the workplace and home of the farming community. Please respect the privacy and work of those who live along the Usk Valley Walk and do not do anything, that might affect livestock, crops or farm machinery.

LOCAL BUSINESSES

Please support local businesses. Every purchase you make during your visit or on your walk, helps local employment and preserves services in the countryside. Use shops, public houses and accommodation services along the route

OTHER WALKS

Newport City Council, Monmouthshire County Council and the Brecon Beacons National Park Authority produce leaflets and booklets describing other walks in and near the Usk Valley. These include walks on the Blorenge, Sugar Loaf and Skirrid mountains near Abergavenny and industrial archaeology trails in the Clydach Gorge. Further information is available from the Tourist Information Centres and from the Brecon Beacons National Park Information Centre in Abergavenny and the National park Mountain Centre at Libanus. The three authorities also provide programmes of guided walks and countryside activities in their respective areas.

Further information about this and other walking and riding publications can be obtained from:

Newport City Council:
Tel 01633 244491
Monmouthshire County Council:
Tel 01633 644858
Brecon Beacons National Park
Authority:Tel 01874 624437
National Park Mountain Centre:
Tel 01874 623366

ACCURACY

Whilst every effort has been made to ensure the accuracy of details given in this publication, it should be remembered the countryside is subject to continuous change. What is accurately described this year may be out of date next year. The publishers cannot accept responsibility for any errors or omissions, nor for any actions taken or not taken, as a result of the information presented.

".....the River Usk
escaped the ravages
of the industrial
Revolution that
for so long blighted
the other rivers of the
South Wales Valleys......"

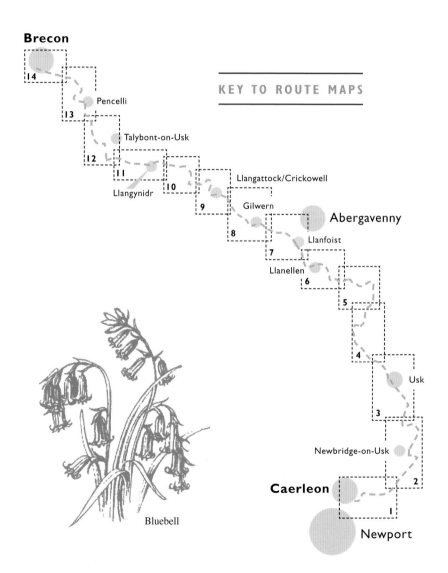

Brecon

14

Pencelli

13

Talybont-on-Usk

12

11

Llangynidr

10

Llangattock/Crickowell

9

Gilwern

8

1

Abergavenny

Llanfoist

7

Llanellen

6

5

4

Usk

3

Newbridge-on-Usk

2

Caerleon

1

Newport

KEY TO ROUTE MAPS

Bluebell

15

The Lower Usk valley

Route summary

There are good views of the southern Usk Valley along this section. Soon after leaving Caerleon, the Walk climbs up the eastern side of the valley and passes along the western edge of Wentwood Forest. It descends at Bertholey, then climbs over the shoulder of Cefn Hill, before dropping down into Llantrisant. The path follows the river to Llanllowell and then uses a B road as far as the outskirts of Usk.

Cowslips

Caerleon

Caerleon stands on the site of the important Roman Legionary fortress of "Isca", originally established and built to subdue the local Silures tribe but later to become one of the three principal bases of Roman occupied Britain.

Substantial remains of the Roman fortress can still be seen at the amphitheatre, the barracks and the site of the bathhouse. A museum in the High Street displays a large number of interesting Roman exhibits found locally and traces the history of the Legionary occupation.

The recent resurgence of interest in the "Knights of the Round Table" has rekindled Caerleon's claim to be the site of "Camelot". Lord Tennyson is said to have drawn inspiration for his poem "The Idylls of the King" from a visit to the amphitheatre, which was known then as King Arthur's Round Table. A wall plaque inside the 16th century Hanbury Arms commemorates his short stay in 1856.

Caerleon was an important port from Roman times through to the Industrial Revolution, when a tramroad for the conveyance of iron and coal led down to a quay by the bridge.

17

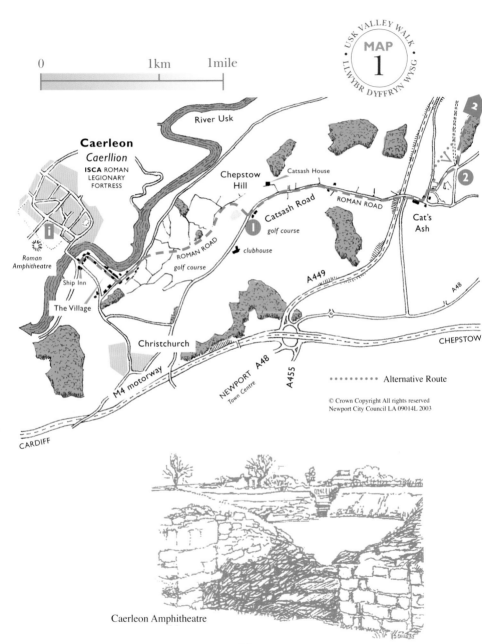

Caerleon Amphitheatre

Leave the Ship Inn and follow the waymarks by turning left through a quiet backwater of Caerleon known locally as the 'old village'. Follow the road round to the right to a T junction opposite the Bell Inn and turn left along the Bulmore road. After three hundred yards turn up a track to the right over a stile and climb through woodland. Looking back you get a good view of the River Usk and the mouth of the River Lwyd.

Carry on up the hill reaching a golf course which is part of the Celtic Manor Resort complex. Turn left and follow the waymarks keeping close to the hedge, then turn right to take you alongside the raised banks of a small reservoir. After a short distance you reach the Cats Ash road. ❶

Turn left and follow the road for about a mile crossing over the dual carriageway (A449) to the hamlet of Cats Ash. Take care along this road as there is fast-moving traffic and it is narrow. Turn left (signpost) and climb the steep rise for 100 yards and turn right at the waymark (just before a house) up a narrow shady track. Follow the track upwards to a metalled road. ❷

Immediately turn left and go through the second of two gates. Carry on through two more gates in

The lower Usk

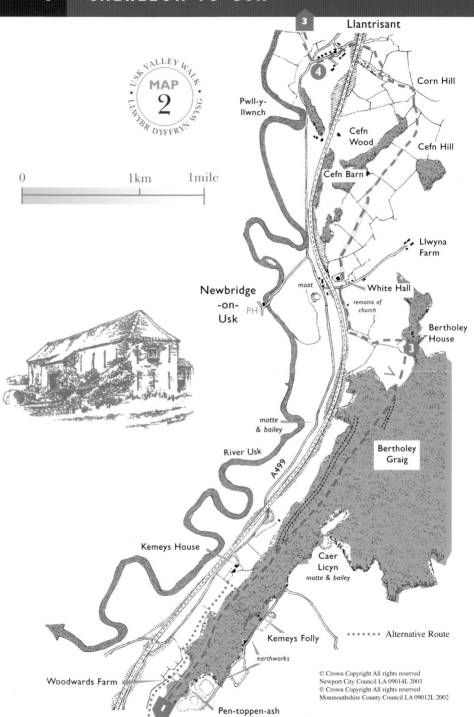

USK VALLEY WALK • LLWYBR DYFFRYN WYSG

MAP 2

0 — 1km — 1mile

Llantrisant

Corn Hill

Pwll-y-llwnch

Cefn Wood

Cefn Hill

Cefn Barn

Llwyna Farm

moat

White Hall

Newbridge-on-Usk

PH

remains of church

Bertholey House

Bertholey Graig

motte & bailey

River Usk

A499

Kemeys House

Caer Licyn
motte & bailey

Kemeys Folly

········· Alternative Route

earthworks

Woodwards Farm

Pen-toppen-ash

quick succession. The next two miles, rising to some 500 ft above the River Usk, are along the western edge of Wentwood. This is a very pretty part of the walk through mixed woodland with occasional but superb glimpses of the Usk Valley below. A short distance along the track there is a fork. Keep to the left and carry on along the path which at first gently undulates and then falls slowly. It then rises and widens a little.

This area is rich in ferns and, apart from the ubiquitous bracken, you can see the Male fern, Lady fern, Narrow and Broad Buckler ferns and the Hart's Tongue fern. Still climbing, the track then widens into a forestry road.

Sweet chestnut trees are seen here and are laden with fruit in the autumn. Carry on climbing, gradually penetrating deeper into Wentwood, past a clump of tall conifers on the left, to a T junction, and, at a large sign, turn abruptly left down a steep narrow track for a short distance to a small gate and stile which lead into an open field. There is an excellent view of the Usk valley from here with Newbridge and Llangibby in the foreground, the hills of the South Wales Valleys to the west, the Brecon Beacons to the north west, the Black Mountains to the north and a glimpse of Usk itself.

Walk directly towards an ancient oak tree at the foot of a deep scoop in the ground and keeping to the same line carry on to the next stile deep under the trees. Cross the next field diagonally to the left to a gate in the corner keeping Bertholey House on the right and turn left along a metalled drive. ❸

BERTHOLEY HOUSE

This rebuilt Georgian mansion is in an enviable location set high on the hill with panoramic views across and along the valley. It was built around 1830 but was largely destroyed by an accidental fire in 1905. It lay derelict for most of the 20th century but major repairs started in 1999. Manor houses have stood on this site since the 13th century. The knights who held this land under the lordship of Usk also held the ferryboat of Brethelly, the ferry being somewhere near Newbridge.

Towards Twmbarlwm

21

Follow the drive down to where it turns right along the side of the dual carriageway. Carry on to a T junction. If the tide is right (details in the Western Mail) its worth while taking a short diversion (1 mile) to Newbridge. This old bridge marks the limit of the tidal reaches of the river. Looking over the bridge downstream its often possible to see salmon and sea trout jumping as the tide comes in. If you're very lucky you may see a shoal of shad following the salmon in and dimpling the surface of the river whilst taking surface food. These are a rare migratory fish and run the rivers Usk and Wye in the spring. There is an inn next to the bridge that has a beer garden overlooking the river.

After a few yards go over a stile on the right-hand side of the road before the road bridge. Follow the hedge on the left to another stile and go slightly right crossing a short stretch of farmyard (White Hall) to yet another one. Follow a well-defined farm track which winds uphill through several fields (access through farm gates - no stiles) past telecom communication masts on the left into a field in the centre of which stands Cefn Barn.

Leave the track, turn right, still climbing, and follow the left-hand edge of the hedge to a gate. Carry on through the gate still following the hedge and still climbing to another gate. Proceed diagonally to the left rising gently to the summit of Cefn Hill then descend, keeping to a mid-point between Cefn Wood on the left and a clump of trees on your right to a gap in the hedge. The faint track becomes more prominent. As you descend there is a good view of the Usk Valley and surrounding hills. Cross the next field diagonally to the right and go through a gate in the corner to a short stretch of shady track and through another gate into an open field.

Newbridge-on-Usk

Llanllowell

Carry on, keeping to the right as far as the corner of the field. There is a gate straight ahead and another gate and stile to the right. Turn left and follow the hedge downhill to a stile on the right immediately followed by a second stile to the left.

Carry on downhill (Corn Hill Cottage to the right) through a field keeping to the left of a lane. About half way down the field take a stile into the lane down steep stone steps. Go straight across into a narrow strip of woodland and follow the waymarks through a field, joining a lane which comes out opposite Llantrisant Church. Turn left onto a surfaced road and go through the village to meet a wider road and turn right. **4**

After 40 yards take a stile across the road and cross the field to a footbridge and follow the hedge on the right. Go through the next gate to the right and carry on in the same direction keeping close to the hedge on the left to a stile which leads into a lane. Carry on for a short distance in the same direction until the lane swings to the left to go to a pumping station. Go straight on following close to the river until it is joined by the Olway Brook. Follow the brook until the path veers to the right to reach Llanllowell via a short lane. **5**

Giant Hogweed

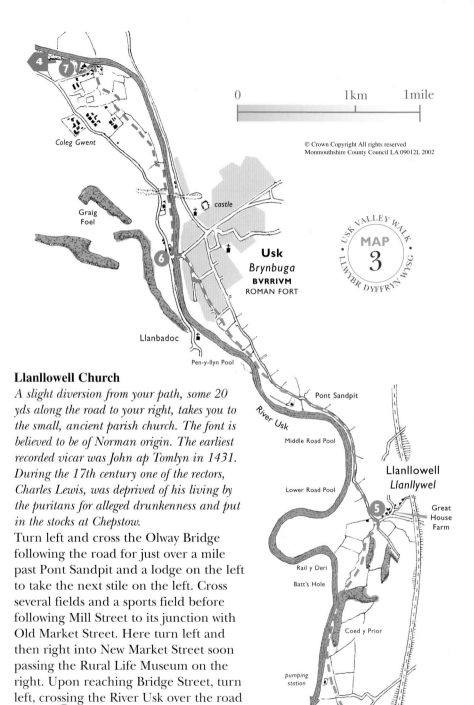

Usk
Brynbuga
BVRRIVM
ROMAN FORT

USK VALLEY WALK · LLWYBR DYFFRYN WYSG

MAP
3

Coleg Gwent

Graig
Foel

castle

Llanbadoc

Pen-y-llyn Pool

Pont Sandpit

River Usk

Middle Road Pool

Lower Road Pool

Llanllowell
Llanllywel

Great
House
Farm

Rail y Deri

Batt's Hole

Coed y Prior

pumping
station

Llanllowell Church

*A slight diversion from your path, some 20
yds along the road to your right, takes you to
the small, ancient parish church. The font is
believed to be of Norman origin. The earliest
recorded vicar was John ap Tomlyn in 1431.
During the 17th century one of the rectors,
Charles Lewis, was deprived of his living by
the puritans for alleged drunkenness and put
in the stocks at Chepstow.*

Turn left and cross the Olway Bridge
following the road for just over a mile
past Pont Sandpit and a lodge on the left
to take the next stile on the left. Cross
several fields and a sports field before
following Mill Street to its junction with
Old Market Street. Here turn left and
then right into New Market Street soon
passing the Rural Life Museum on the
right. Upon reaching Bridge Street, turn
left, crossing the River Usk over the road
bridge. **6**

Pant-y-Goitre

Route summary

You are never far away from the river along this undulating, but generally level section. Heading north from Usk on the west bank, the walk uses mainly field paths on its way to Chain Bridge. Here it crosses the river to follow a delightful route along the east bank to Clytha Park (National Trust). Now heading west, the walk keeps mainly through river meadows passing small settlements at The Bryn and Llanover, before arriving at Llanellen.

Nettleleaved
Bellflower

Usk

Nestling beside the river that gave it its name, this small historic market town and famous angling centre merits time to explore.
One of the oldest towns in Wales its history is recorded back to Roman times. They established the legionary fort of Burrium here in 55 AD before moving to their new fort at Caerleon (Isca) in 75AD.
The Normans settled in the area soon after the Conquest and by the 12th century had turned the town into a stronghold with a castle, a Benedictine Priory and a mediaeval street plan that largely survives through to this day.
Gaining its charter in 1398 from Roger Mortimer, Earl of March, Usk continued to thrive as an agricultural market town. It was always prone to flooding and inevitably frequently caught up in the border disputes between the English and the Welsh.
Destroyed by the Glyndwr Rebellion in 1402, the townspeople subsequently, in 1405 witnessed the defeat of Glyndwr's forces at a site just above the castle.
During the Civil War, the Parliamentary Army briefly captured Usk.
With its sixteen pubs, restaurants and

hotels, modern Usk provides an excellent base for walkers wishing to explore the area.

Having crossed the road bridge, turn right and then climb the steps over the flood wall to the right and go down to a surfaced path above the river which leads to the Island (a mis-named park-like picnic and recreation area). Carry on by the river passing under the old railway bridge where the path becomes more distinct. After about 300 yards turn left through a gate and follow the right-hand edge of the field as it veers away from the river. Keep ahead along the edge of the field until reaching the far corner next to fence on the left.

JAPANWARE

From the late 18th century and through to the 19th century, Usk became well known for the quality of its Japanware. In the early 18th century, Thomas Allgood developed the process of applying a lacquer to tinplate that was durable, heatproof and inexpensive and by 1735 Pontypool was famous for its production. Examples of Japanware can be seen at The Valley Inheritance Museum, Pontypool.

The Allgood family held close the secret of the enamelling process. In 1761 a family dispute resulted in two of the sons setting up a rival factory in New Market Street, Usk.

Usk

Follow the path through a small plantation,with the stream on the right and a fence on the left to arrive at a hunting gate leading onto a tarmac lane. Turn right, cross a tractor bridge and then turn left into a rugby field. Keep to the left by a smaller brook (tributary of the larger one) to a stile in the left-hand corner of the field followed immediately by another to the right. The path is not obvious here.

Cut diagonally to the left across the field to a stile in the corner. This leads into a narrow stretch of path with a landscaped water garden and fountains to the right (Prioress Mill).

PRIORESS MILL
This 16th century mill was one of the last water powered corn mills to operate in the county. The Berthin Brook, a tributary of the River Usk provided the motive power.

After passing Prioress Mill, bear left on to a surfaced lane until you pass an electricity sub-station. **7**

Turn right through a kissing gate and follow the right hand edge of the field to the corner, ignoring the stile ahead, and turn left. Keep to the right hand edge and go through two more fields climbing gently all the time. The river below has now swung to the right in a large loop.

Pass into another field and after a while drop down to a farm track on the right and through a farm gate onto a minor road. Turn right and follow the road round to the left past Great Estavarney Farm on the right.

GREAT ESTAVARNEY
For some 300 years between the 13th - 15th century Cistercian monks from Tintern Abbey worked the land around this farm.

After about half a mile's climb take a well-marked stile to the right **8**. Climb the rise, bearing slightly to the left (the path is not at all obvious here) and drop down to a stile in the

Usk Castle

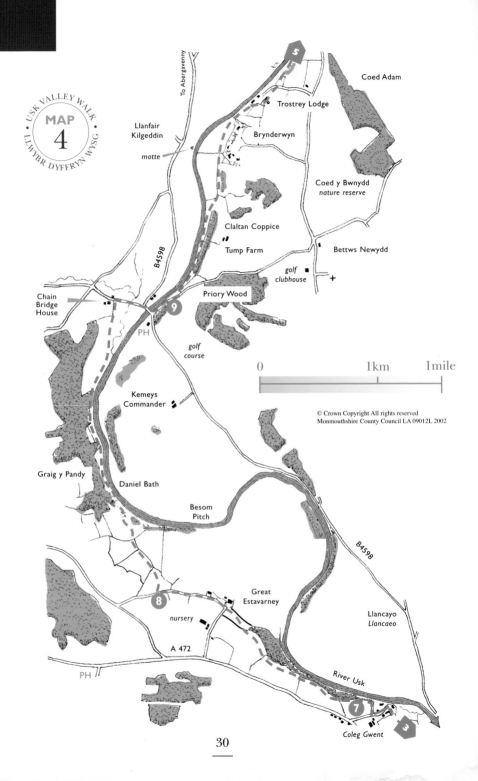

Coed Adam

To Abergavenny

Trostrey Lodge

USK VALLEY WALK

MAP 4

LLWYBR DYFFRYN WYSG

Llanfair Kilgeddin

Brynderwyn

motte

Coed y Bwnydd
nature reserve

Claltan Coppice

Tump Farm

Bettws Newydd

golf clubhouse

Chain Bridge House

Priory Wood

9

PH

golf course

Kemeys Commander

0   1km   1mile

© Crown Copyright All rights reserved
Monmouthshire County Council LA 09012L 2002

Graig y Pandy

Daniel Bath

Besom Pitch

B4598

Great Estavarney

8

nursery

Llancayo
Llancaeo

A 472

PH

River Usk

7

3

Coleg Gwent

far left-hand corner of the field ignoring the gate on the left. Go through the next two fields close to the fence on the right. There is a good view of Skirrid to the north. After the next stile there is a hillock straight ahead. Skirt this to the right following the contours and, after passing two beech trees to the right, cross a stile and take a good track down through woodland to join a larger track and bear left.

By the pumping station you are standing on the oldest exposed rocks in Gwent, some 430 million years old.

After a few yards turn right on to a narrow track leading to a stile and rejoin the river bank. This is a very pretty section of the walk. Carry on past a fisherman's hut to a stile, into a short stretch of woodland and over a stile into a field. Carry on, meeting and following a brook which empties into the river, and through a farm gate on to a wide track leading past Chain Bridge House. Pass through two farm gates on to a road and turn right to Chainbridge **9** where there is a pub and restaurant.

After crossing the bridge turn left (waymarked and signposted to Bettws Newydd), climb the hill for about 1/4 mile. Turn left over a stile and take a waymarked path running towards the river (also signposted Clytha Park).

Descend steeply to a kissing gate at river level. Carry on through two small wooden gates, along the edge of a wood, Claltan Coppice, eventually reaching an open field.

Cross a small brook and pass through a farm gate. Follow the path with patchy woodland on the right and over a stile by a ruined barn, over another brook and through a kissing gate into a large park-like field passing Brynderwyn (an imposing country house) on the right. Go through a kissing gate leading into a field.

Follow the path uphill, to a kissing gate at the top on the right. Keeping left go through a farm gate, skirt round the left-hand side of Trostrey Lodge and, after a few yards, meet a lane. After 50 yards turn left through a wooden gate when you will soon find a very welcome wooden seat thoughtfully provided by the Monmouth Footpath Volunteers. You can look down on the river through the trees whilst having that well-earned rest.

TROSTREY FORGE

Where the river is narrowed by rocks at Trostrey, once stood the Trostrey Forge - taking advantage of the water power and adjacent sources of charcoal but dependent on distant supplies of iron ore, probably from Blaenafon.

Carry on over a stile into a field keeping to the left and descending to another stile, which leads into a steep section through woodland to a stile by the river.

Follow the river and negotiate an awkward ditch and carry on to a footbridge over a small brook. Still following the river, go through a large open field to a kissing gate leading onto a wide track. Bear left into National Trust land, which is liberally provided with benches, to a stile (complete with dog flap) which leads into woodland. Go over a footbridge and then through a wooden gate onto the B4598 ⑩.

CLYTHA PARK

This was mainly laid out in the 1790s by John Davenport, a landscape gardener from Shropshire for the owner William Jones the elder. It contained many fine specimen trees, woodland plantations, shrubberies, gardens, lawns and a lake bounded by yew trees. A large brick walled kitchen garden with hothouses was situated close to the house.

CLYTHA HOUSE

The present neo-classical house was built of Bath stone between 1821 and 1824 by Edward Haycock of Shrewsbury for William Jones the younger. It stands on the site of an earlier Georgian brick house.

Clytha Castle

CLYTHA CASTLE FOLLY

This was built as an "eye-catcher" from Clytha House in 1790. It is now leased to the Landmark Trust who let it out for holiday accommodation. Clytha Park and Castle were acquired by the National Trust in 1979.

Turn left along the road, pass the drive leading to the Llansantffraed Court Hotel (food, drink and accommodation) and take the next road left. Carry on to a T junction, turn left and after 100 yards, just before Pant y Goitre bridge **11**, take a gate on the right.

From this attractive old bridge you can see the late 18th century mansion, a fine example of neo-classical design dating from the "Romantic" period.

Follow the river for 100 yards over a stile and keep to the hedge on the right, taking you away from the river, until it swings to the right past a house. Keep to the same line as before and cross the large field to a stile in the far corner.

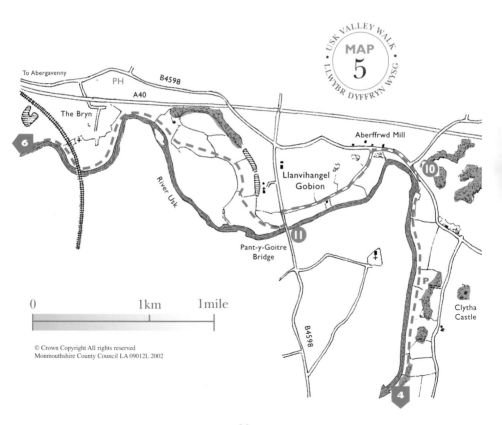

On the left is a series of marshy ponds nestling in an old course of the river. Keeping the fence to your left carry on through 3 more fields to meet the river again. Cross a stile and go through two more fields to a footbridge on the fringe of The Bryn.

Bryns abound in Wales, for the name means bank or hill, but this one is a small village that as recently as the turn of the century stood on the bank of the river.
The church, which is dedicated to St Cadoc was built alongside the river but now, like the village of the Bryn, is separated from it by 500 yds of meadows. The remains of a late medieval cross stand beyond the north side of the church and opposite the entrance porch is a rare example of a "kneeling stone".
Straight on is another footbridge. A half-mile diversion from this point will take you to the King of Prussia pub where there is excellent food and drink.

Follow the river under a railway bridge to the next stile. Go straight on for about 400 yards to a group of four large trees. Bear slightly right away from the river to a stile in the fence facing. Keep towards the fence on the right and walk back to the river past a low circular building, a wartime pillbox, to a footbridge over the main river at Llanover. This is private and is not available for walkers to cross ⑫. On the other side of the river, adjacent to the bridge, is a very attractive old cottage cum boathouse - Tyr Afon. A stream runs through an archway under the cottage into the river.

Turn to the right, cross a stile and follow the river through three fields and carry on through a narrower shaded stretch, with a steep bank to the right, to a footbridge opposite Glan Usk Farm. Otters are often seen here in the late evening and early morning. Climb steeply up wooden steps to a field, turn left and keep to the edge of the woodland on the left as it follows the bends of the river, slowly dropping down to a stile.

Carry on through the field to two more stiles in quick succession and on to a footbridge. From here make directly for Llanellen Bridge which is now in view and go on to the A4042 through a metal kissing gate. Turn left and carefully cross the bridge into Llanellen. The bridge is narrow, there is no footpath, and the road is very busy ⑬. There is a convenient café for walkers behind the post office.

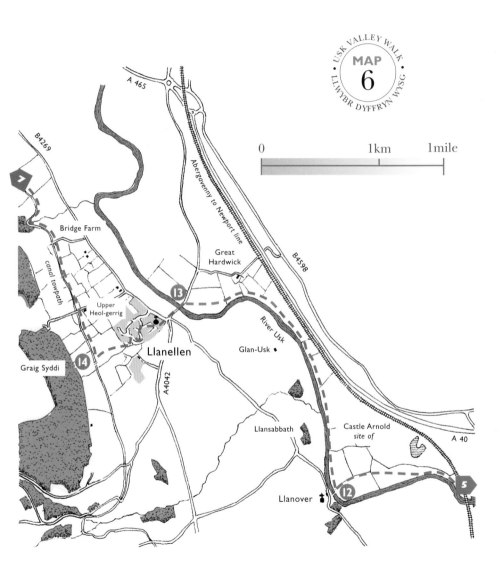

USK VALLEY WALK
MAP
6
LLWYBR DYFFRYN WYSG

A 465

B4269

7

Abergavenny to Newport line

0   1km   1mile

Bridge Farm

canal towpath

Great Hardwick

B4598

13

Upper Heol-gerrig

River Usk

Llanellen

Glan-Usk

14

Graig Syddi

A4042

Llansabbath

Castle Arnold
site of

A 40

Llanover

12

5

Near Llanelly

Route summary

Apart from the short uphill start from Llanellen, the whole of this section keeps on the level, following the towpath of the Monmouthshire and Brecon Canal. Not only is this a very scenic walk, offering fine views across the Usk Valley towards the Sugar Loaf, Skirrid and Black Mountains, but it is full of reminders from the industrial revolution. There are several hostelries along the towpath, happy to cater for the needs of walkers.

Balm leaved Figwort

Llanellen

Llanellen does not now have an inn, though once it had three. Lady Llanover, the wife of Sir Benjamin Hall of "Big Ben" fame, on whose estate the village lay, closed two of the taverns and turned the third into a temperance house called Y Seren Gobaith (the Star of Hope). She disliked "strong drink".
The church is 12th century and in its graveyard are the graves of ten of Cromwell's soldiers who died whilst camped nearby during the Civil War. The old vicarage was once the home of Alexander Cordell author of 'Rape of the Fair Country'.

After traversing the Llanellen road bridge, cross the road and take the next road to the right (information board on the right hand side). After a few yards carefully cross the Llanfoist road and walk up St Helen's Close which is straight ahead and enter St Helen's churchyard. Leave the churchyard through a kissing gate leading on to Ashgrove. Continue ahead for 50 metres and turn left at the junction with Elm Drive. Follow the road round for 200 metres, then turn left at 40 Elm Drive up the short cul-de-sac, to join a tarmac path round the side and back garden of No 48. Where this path ends, turn right through a kissing gate into the field and then continue uphill, keeping the fence on your left, until you reach a bridle gate in the hedge at the top of the ⑭ field. Looking back and to the north, there is an excellent view of the Gavenny Valley. This is embraced by Skirrid Fach (Little Skirrid) and Skirrid Fawr (Big Skirrid) to the east and Llanwenarth Breast, Rholben and the Sugar Loaf to the west with a glimpse of other hills of the Black Mountains in between. One could imagine that Abergavenny had been poured into the head of the Valley,

gradually spreading out as it approached the River Usk. Turn to the right and follow the canal towpath past Bridge Farm to a sharp bend where a stream flows under the waterway. A branch of the stream feeds water into the canal.

There are a number of streams running under the canal and, where the terrain is steep, the canal turns sharply into the hillside following the erosion of the rock. On Bridge No 95 note the presence of the Rustyback Fern, a lover of limestone and mortar. Other related ferns in the same position are the Maidenhair Spleenwort and Wall Rue. The latter two are present on many of the bridges together with the ivy-leaved toadflax.

Go on to Llanfoist ⑮ the nearest point to Abergavenny on the walk. Here is a boatyard and convenient bench. The wharf marked the end of Hill's tramway which, skirting around the Blorenge, linked the ironworks at Blaenavon and Garnddyrys Forge.

One of the most interesting sites on the canal is the complex at Llanfoist where an incline that served Hills tramroad (built in 1818) terminates at a warehouse and loading wharf. The trackbed of the tramroad is easily

Fishing Kingfisher

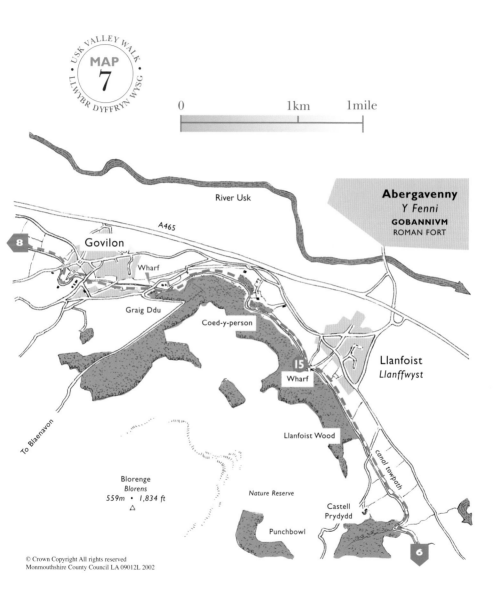

USK VALLEY WALK · LLWYBR DYFFRYN WYSG

MAP 7

0   1km   1mile

River Usk

A465

Abergavenny
Y Fenni
GOBANNIVM
ROMAN FORT

8

Govilon

Wharf

Graig Ddu

Coed-y-person

15

Wharf

Llanfoist
Llanffwyst

To Blaenavon

Llanfoist Wood

canal towpath

Blorenge
Blorens
559m • 1,834 ft
△

Nature Reserve

Punchbowl

Castell
Prydydd

6

followed as it climbs sharply up the Blorenge Mountain before levelling out to pass underneath the site of an iron forge, opened in 1816. Clinging tenaciously to the hillside it then sweeps around the head of the valley into limestone quarries. Before passing through a 1 1/2 mile tunnel (now blocked) to Blaenafon, where the remains of the ironworks and the Big Pit Mining Museum are popular visitor attractions.

Carrying on you pass a fine beech wood on the steep hillside, one of several in this area. This stretch is full of bends as the canal follows the contours of the hill. You soon come

to a bench on which to rest and an adjacent mileage sign. At bridge No 96 cross the canal and enter Govilon

Like many villages in this part of Gwent, Govilon was largely agricultural before the 18th century Industrial Revolution and the coming of the canal, and later the railway. By the middle of the 19th century there were 19 public houses to meet the demand of local and passing trade. Now, but two remain.

One of the oldest buildings is Llanwenarth chapel. Built in 1695, it was the first Baptist chapel to be built in Wales. The graveyard backs onto the canal and it was the custom to convey the corpses by barge for burial.

Towards Crickhowell

Canal at Llangattock

On the opposite bank is a residential area with several pretty canal-side gardens and after the next bridge is a large private mooring belonging to the Govilon Boat Club. Just before an unnumbered railway bridge is an information board. The intricate brickwork of the archway is well-worth examination.

Cross back over the canal at bridge No 98. A quarter of a mile diversion down the road will take you to the Lion Inn (food and accommodation). Continuing along the canal cross a stream and, shortly, go down steep steps to a road leading to the Bridgend Inn (food and a boules court!) a hundred yards away. If you're self-sufficient there is a convenient bench nearby.

After bridge No 101 the canal goes under the Heads of the Valleys road (A465), the road following the canal to Gilwern where there is a mooring and two pubs offering food, The Bridgend Inn (yes, another one) on the near side and, opposite, The Navigation Inn **16** .

GILWERN

Work started on the canal started here in 1797, a massive earth bank being constructed to form an aqueduct across the River Clydach, which joins the Usk a mile further down stream.

A network of tramroads brought coal, lime and the products of the ironworks in the Clydach Gorge to lime kilns and

wharves on the canal. The lime was transported to the agricultural areas of Breckonshire whilst the coal and iron were conveyed to the industrial centres in South Wales and to Newport docks. The Clydach Gorge is an industrial archaeologist's paradise. This 3 1/2 by 1/2 mile cleft is crammed with the remains of charcoal and coke burning iron furnaces, lime kilns and quarries, tramroads, the trackbed of the Merthyr Tydfil and Abergavenny Railway, a cast iron bridge dated 1824 and industrial housing.

Leave Gilwern and follow the canal over an embankment, under which flows the River Clydach. The canal sweeps round a bend with an overflow on the opposite bank, to a boatyard (Gilwern Narrowboats). There are many feeder streams flowing into the canal with, at intervals, weirs which keep the water at a constant level. Just after the next bridge is the Gilwern Wharf picnic site with handy benches and tables. The Rustyback Fern decorates bridge No 105. This is a very pretty stretch going through woodland much of the way to Llangattock.

You come out of the woodland as you approach Pen-pedair-heol Farm by bridge No 110. Between here and the

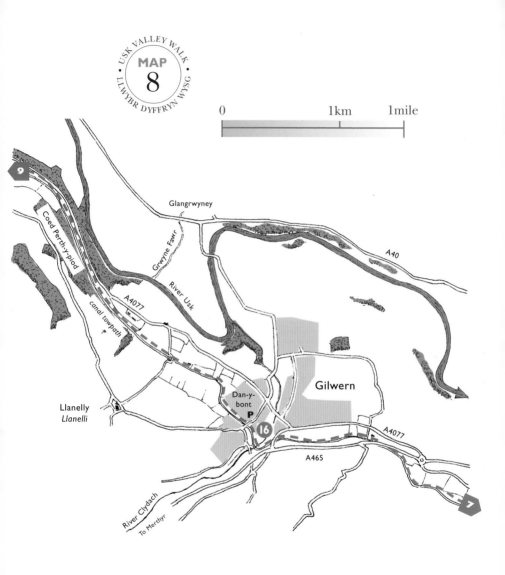

USK VALLEY WALK · LLWYBR DYFFRYN WYSG

MAP 8

0   1km   1mile

9

Glangrwyney

Coed Perth-y-pîod

Grwyne Fawr

River Usk

A40

A4077

canal towpath

Dan-y-bont
P

Gilwern

Llanelly
Llanelli

16

A4077

A465

River Clydach

To Merthyr

7

next two bridges are excellent views of the Black Mountains to the right and the lower slopes of the Brecon Beacons across the water to the left. Just after bridge No 113, by the towpath, is a very fine redwood tree. It measures about 20 ft across at the base including the bolstering roots and the main trunk above has a diameter of about 8 ft. The Wellingtonia (Sequoiadendron giganteum) is a native of the western Sierras of California and can attain a height of 365 ft (110m) and live to 4,000 years. This specimen is certainly over 100 years old but, surprisingly, not more than 150 as the seeds first reached Britain in the 1850s. It is thought that the mild Usk Valley climate has contributed to the very rapid growth.

There is a long bend to the right passing Llangattock Park House and after the next bridge No 114, you enter the outskirts of Llangattock with two lime kilns sunk into the hillside on the opposite bank.

Crickhowell Bridge

44

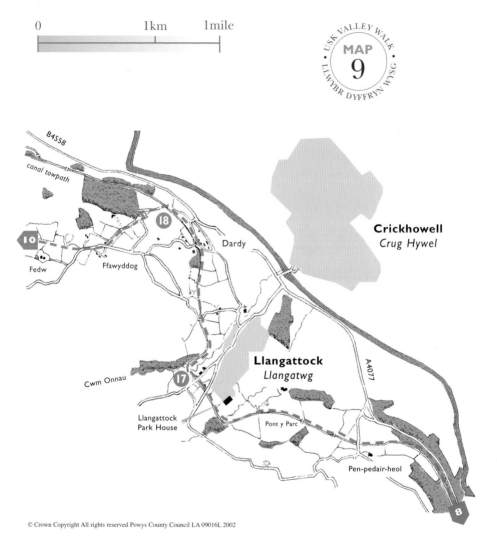

0   1km   1mile

USK VALLEY WALK
MAP
9
LLWYBR DYFFRYN WYSG

B4558

canal towpath

10

Fedw

Ffawyddog

18

Dardy

Crickhowell
Crug Hywel

Cwm Onnau

17

Llangattock
Llangatwg

A4077

Llangattock
Park House

Pont y Parc

Pen-pedair-heol

8

Gliffaes through the trees

Route summary

Soon after leaving Llangattock, the walk leaves the canal to climb steeply up the hillside, in contrast to the previous level walk in Section 3. The path drops down to rejoin the canal just short of Llangynidr. If time is at a premium, the canal can be followed all the way to Brecon from here. Beyond Llangynidr, there is a strenuous uphill section, the path reaching 1,000 ft, with good views, before dropping down an old mountain tramway, past Talybont Reservoir, to the village of Aber.

Llangattock

The village takes its name from the Celtic saint, Cattwg, a 6th century contemporary of St David. The parish church of St Cadoc's was established in the 6th century, the present building dating from the 12th century.

The large and well-preserved limestone kilns at the edge of the canal and the adjacent wharf were built during the early 19th century to facilitate the manufacture and transportation of lime.

Llangattock was also an important weaving centre, a true cottage industry that was once carried out in some of the older houses bordering the narrow streets of the village.

The next bridge in Llangattock (No 115) leads to a wharf ⓱ . Ty Croeso Hotel some 100 yards from bridge No 118 provides for food, drink and accommodation.

Dame's Violet

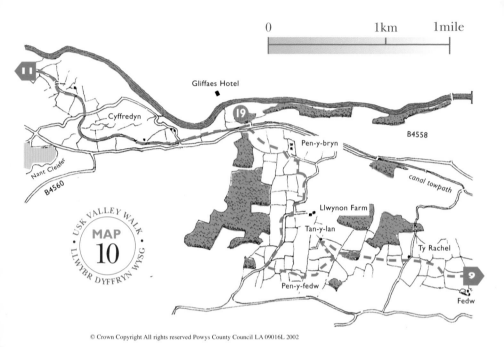

CRICKHOWELL

This interesting little market town by the side of the River Usk can be seen in the valley, one mile below Llangattock.Its name is derived from the Iron Age Fort, Crug Hywel (Howell's Cairn) set on the summit of Table Mountain, some 1,481 ft up above the town. This ancient stronghold is said to be the home of the 9th century King Hywel Dda, the first king to lay down laws for the government of the Welsh.

The buildings in Crickhowell span some seven centuries and the streets of the town are full of interesting architecture. One of the town's most intriguing constructions is the bridge over the Usk, known to have been in existence in 1538 but rebuilt in 1706. Built in local stone, it can be a little disconcerting, having 13 arches on one side and 12 on the other - the result of alterations made in 1830.

The town was the birthplace and home of Sir George Everest, surveyor general of India from 1830-41, who in 1841 first recorded the location and height of Mount Everest.

Gliffaes

At bridge 119 ⑱ we leave the canal towpath to rejoin it at Bridge No 125. Cross the bridge and keeping to the left of the waymark post climb steeply up through woodland along a stony bridleway. Ignore the well-marked path ahead and keep to the bridleway which veers sharply to the left and, shortly, to the right. As is the case with most of the woodland adjacent to the canal there is a wealth of ferns. Keep on climbing steeply until you come out of the woodland (Cae

College Farm on the right) and on to a surfaced lane leading to the outskirts of Ffawyddog.

Just past the Old Sunday School, turn right at a T junction and go up a wider road until it swings left opposite the entrance to Penffawyddog. Leave the road and carry straight on, crossing a stile into a field. Following the fence on the right gently uphill, but gradually veering to the left, you come to two stiles in the right hand corner of the field. Take the one facing you.

Carry on through the centre of the field until you meet a fence on the right and follow this to a stile which leads on to a farm track. Cross this and another stile into a field, keeping the fence on the right hand side. Cross another stile and carry straight on, slightly downhill, through the centre of a field, through a line of trees and a derelict stone wall, to a stile in the right hand corner. Go across the next field to a stile in the corner. Cross this and pass between two old barns, keeping slightly to the right after the second one to a farm gate.

Go through this and over a brook, to a line of trees where there is another brook. Carry on downhill to another farm gate and keeping slightly to the left go up to a stone building. Stay on its left and after a few yards take a stile in the fence on the left. Continue in the same direction gradually climbing the hillside on a faint track, crossing a wide track. A much better track continues straight on and you soon join another one coming in from the left.

Drop down to a stile leading into a lane. Turn immediately left up the lane climbing steeply. The lane swings sharply to the right and meets a farm gate leading into a steeply sloping field. Follow the directional sign up the field to the top right hand corner, over a broken stone wall to a stile. Go across to the right hand corner of the field to meet a fence coming in from the right. Cross the stile and climb up the hill to meet a farm track going to Pen-y-fedw. Bear right and follow the track down to meet another wider track. Keep to the left and continue downhill to a gate leading to a steep stony lane.

Turn right and carry on for about 1/2 mile to a surfaced lane just before Llwynon Farm. Turn left and carry on downhill and, where the lane swings to the right, take a stile on the left. Follow the fence on the left and, where it goes off to the left carry straight on to the far corner of the field.

Take a stile onto a surfaced lane and turn left, through a farm gate, past Pen-y-bryn Farm on the right and cross the stile straight ahead into a field. Go diagonally through the field to a stile in the far corner and into the next field bearing right to a stile in the middle of the fence facing and climb carefully down steps to see a road ahead, with the canal adjacent and the River Usk down in the valley below. Turn left and immediately right to cross bridge No 125 and rejoin the canal **19** .

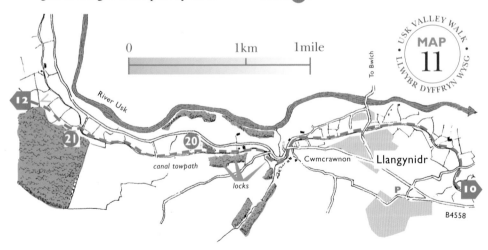

Llangynidr Bridge

Gliffaes House (now a hotel) can be seen through the trees across the river between bridges 125 and 126. From bridge 129 it is 1/2 mile to the village of Llangynidr and the Red Lion Inn (food, drink and accommodation). The Parish Church was founded in the 6th century and restored in 1875 and 1929.

A few hundred yards down the road from bridge No 131, the River Usk is crossed by a picturesque old bridge (c1600).
This 7 ft wide crossing spans an attractive stretch of the river and it is well worth a visit

Carrying on there are excellent views of the countryside in all directions. Bridge 132 is immediately followed by lower lock No 64, the first of a series of five locks. The Coach and Horses (food, drink and accommodation) is close by bridge No 133. The approach to the next few bridges is very pleasant and there are a number of benches and picnic tables along the locks. There are moorings and another lock (No 65) and an information board between bridges 133 and 134 where there is a small boatyard.

Soon you come to the final 3 locks of the Llangynidr system with a pond on the right hand side, picnic tables and benches **20** .

Continue along the towpath to bridge No 138.

Llangynidr Locks

Above Talybont Reservoir

At this point we again leave the canal to rejoin it later. Cross the bridge **21** and take the bridle road to the right through a wooden gate into Forestry Commission land to a stile by a small gate leading into an open field. Go straight across until it funnels into woodland and after a few yards of shady track go through a gate and climb up steeply into a field. Cross in the same direction and go through a gate in the fence facing. Looking back there is a good view of the Sugarloaf and the Black Mountains to the north of it. You now start moving away from the canal below you on the right.

Carry on keeping fairly close to the fence on the right, go through a gate still staying close to the fence, and about half way across the field veer to the left to a gap in a line of conifers. Go through a gate and follow a shallow valley on the right still climbing. There is a very good view of the Black Mountains to the east. Climb a stile and follow the bridlepath to a metalled road.

Turn right and after a few yards just before a cattle grid, take a stile to the left into a field and bear slightly left to a gate in the centre of the fence ahead. Go downwards slightly left to

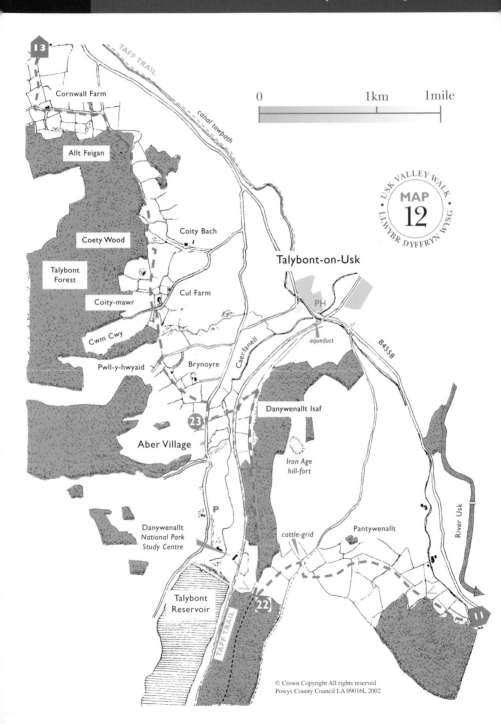

13

Cornwall Farm

TAFF TRAIL

canal towpath

Allt Feigan

0   1km   1mile

Coity Bach

Coety Wood

Talybont-on-Usk

USK VALLEY WALK
MAP
12
LLWYBR DYFFRYN WYSG

Talybont
Forest

Cul Farm

PH

Coity-mawr

Cwm Cwy

aqueduct

B4558

Pwll-y-hwyaid

Brynoyre

Caerfanell

23

Danywenallt Isaf

Aber Village

Iron Age
hill-fort

River Usk

P

Danywenallt
*National Park
Study Centre*

cattle-grid

Pantywenallt

22

Talybont
Reservoir

TAFF TRAIL

11

the bottom left-hand corner of the next field. There is an excellent view of Talybont Reservoir. Beyond you get your first view of the Brecon Beacons with the Pen-y-Fan massif straight ahead.

Cross a stile down to an old tramway and turn right **22**. Just below the dam, rhododendrons are a blaze of colour in shades of red, pink and white in the late spring. Go downhill through pretty mixed woodland. After 1/2 mile the Taff Trail coming in from the left joins the track. Carry on downwards for another 1/2 mile and turn left over a stile.

(A less energetic option here is to carry on down the tramway to Talybont village and then take the canal towpath to Brecon. There are several interesting drawbridges along this section.)

TALYBONT-ON-USK

In the past the village was an important junction of commercial routes. The Brynoer Tramroad brought limestone around Llangynidr Mountain from Trefil Quarry, some seven miles away near Tredegar. The Merthyr & Brecon Railway later followed a parallel course along the Caerfanell valley. The course of this disused railway line now forms part of the long distance path from Cardiff to Brecon, the 'Taff Trail'. On 8

December 1994 heavy rain caused a build up of water draining off the hills into the canal and water was noticed to be leaking from the embankment above the village. The police evacuated people from nearby houses just in time, for before anything could be done to stop the leak, the canal bank collapsed leaving a gap 30 ft wide. Half a million gallons of water and the earth from the bank rushed down the main street.

Go down steeply to an open field staying on the left and turning left at the bottom to meet a kissing gate. Turn left on to a disused railway line and after a few yards right through a metal farm gate. Descend under an old railway bridge and go straight on to another kissing gate crossing a track in doing so. Go steeply down some wooden steps to a further kissing gate leading into a field.

Follow the directional arrow across the field and drop down to a solid footbridge over the River Caerfanell. Turn left and after a few yards take a stile into a field. Follow the right-hand edge to a stile in the bottom right-hand corner of the field onto a narrow but busy road on the outskirts of Aber village and turn right. **23**

Above Llangynidr

Route summary

Leaving Aber, the walk again climbs uphill, passing through several areas of attractive woodland, and offering good views of the Black Mountains, before descending to rejoin the canal at Pencelli. The canal and river soon come close with the canal crossing the Usk over Brynich Viaduct. As you approach the outskirts of Brecon, the valley widens out, and the walk ends at Probert Basin.

Leaving the outskirts of Aber, carry on for 200 yards and turn left through a farm gate up a stream bed and through a good gate into a field. Climb up to the far right-hand corner and cross a stile. Keep fairly close to the hedge on the left-hand side to a stile in the left-hand corner of the field. Pass a small duck pond on the right and Pwll-y-hwyaid farm, with a good view of the Brecon Beacons ahead and the Black Mountains to the right. Cross a stile to a metalled lane and after 70 yards turn left over another stile into a field signposted Coity-Mawr. In the breeding season you can hear the cries of peacocks ahead.

Keep to the left and drop down steep wooden steps to a stream. After crossing a footbridge and a stile to the left climb up through mixed woodland. In the spring this area is full of wild flowers (bluebells, ragged robin, yellow dead nettle, and wood anemones) and ferns. Climb steeply out of the little valley up wooden steps to a magnificent ancient oak tree adjacent to the next stile. Follow the path up to a clearing with Coity-Mawr and a walled garden on the left where the source of the sound of peacocks

Toothwort
and Sycamore

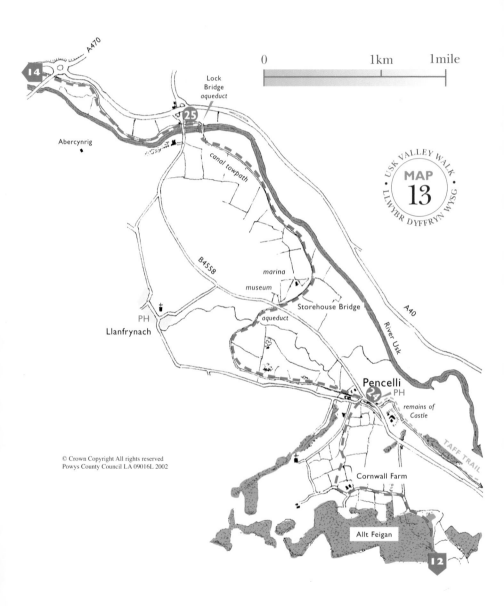

0   1km   1mile

A470

14

Lock
Bridge
aqueduct

25

Abercynrig

canal towpath

· USK VALLEY WALK ·
MAP
13
LLWYBR DYFFRYN WYSG

B4558

marina
museum

Storehouse Bridge

aqueduct

PH
Llanfrynach

A40

River Usk

Pencelli
PH
24

*remains of
Castle*

TAFF TRAIL

Cornwall Farm

Allt Feigan

12

becomes obvious. Cross a stile into a lane and turn left (signposted Pencelli).

Climbing for 50 yards carry straight on leaving the surfaced lane which swings to the right, over a stile (sign to Pencelli). In a few yards turn right and follow a line of particularly fine trees (field maples and horse chestnut are outstanding) with Cui Farm on the right. Cross a stile and carry on down across a small stream to a stile. Follow the fence on the left on the edge of woodland with wild cherries in abundance, ignoring a stile to the left and go through a picturesque old coppiced beech wood leading to a stile.

Carry on through boggy woodland and take a stile to the left into a conifer wood. Ignore the well-trodden path carrying straight on. Carry on through mixed woodland to a stile. Keep to the left and follow the edge of the woodland across a field over a stile.

Keep to the left and take a stile into woodland by a derelict building to meet a deeply rutted lane. Turn right. Follow the lane downwards for about half a mile to a crossroads and turn left on to a stony lane signposted to St Meugan's Church. Carry on passing through Cornwall farm and after 100 yards take a stile to the right into a

Canal Museum

Brynich Aqueduct

field. Go straight on, through several fields, following a stream down through a very pretty valley to meet the B4558. Turn right and then left over bridge No 154 to rejoin the canal at Pencelli. **24**

Just before bridge No 158 at Storehouse is the Waterfolk Canal Museum and teashop with moorings alongside. Situated on the canal-side it offers an insight into the history of the canals in the UK with exhibits and audio-visual presentations. Coming up to bridge No 159 at Ty Newydd are more moorings and the Cambrian Cruisers marina on the other side.

The course of the canal progressively converges with that of the river some 30 feet below. At Millbrook, just before bridge No 161 the weir can be clearly heard and the old mill, close to a fast flowing, very scenic, stretch of the river can be glimpsed through the trees.

Leave the towpath at bridge No 162, exit through a gate, cross the bridge and rejoin the towpath on the other side after passing through another gate. There is a good view of the Brecon Beacons from here including Pen-y-Fan.

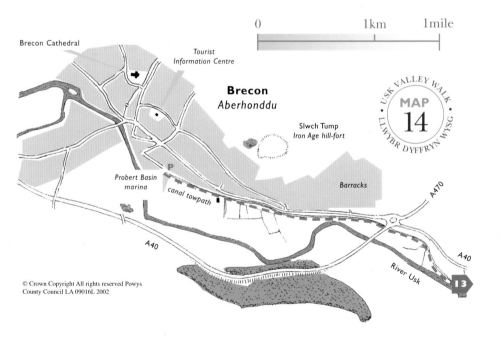

Brecon Cathedral

Tourist Information Centre

Brecon
Aberhonddu

Slwch Tump
Iron Age hill-fort

USK VALLEY WALK
LLWYBR DYFFRYN WYSG
MAP
14

0   1km   1mile

Probert Basin marina

canal towpath

Barracks

A470

A40

River Usk

A40

13

The canal now sweeps to the right and crosses the river over the fine stone built Brynich Aqueduct 25 before turning left and following the course of the river again. The aqueduct passes high over the River Usk allowing views up and down stream and giving some indication of how turbulent the river can be at times of high rainfall.

There are moorings up to the Llanfrynach road **25** at bridge No 163. Looking back there is an excellent view of the aqueduct. Lock No 69 is immediately behind the bridge and there are picnic tables on the canal bank to the left and more moorings. After about 1/2 mile

Abercynrig, a small but beautiful manor house, can be seen on the other side of the river.

As you approach the outskirts of Brecon a large castleated building is seen on your right. This is Brecon Barracks the home of the South Wales Borderers and the Monmouthshire Regimental Museum.

The walk ends after bridge No 166 at the very attractive Probert Basin, some 1/4 mile from the centre of town and the end of the canal. A theatre and restaurant complex are recent additions to the facilities here.

Brecon

century friary. Its present structure is mainly Victorian in Gothic style but some of the old buildings remain.

Sections of the encircling old town walls can still be seen, running up the incline from the Honddu past the Deanery where Charles I slept in 1645, and round to the old monastic gateway.

Brecon is a lively town full of shops, restaurants, pubs and an excellent Tourist Information Centre. The annual Jazz Festival is held in August and attracts top musicians from around the world.

Brecon

This market town, whose history stretches back to the 12th century and beyond, is situated on the north-eastern tip of the Brecon Beacons National Park, where the River Honddu flows into the Usk.

Among the remains of its ancient history is the impressive Priory of St John the Evangelist. Built on the site of a Norman church in the 13th and 14th century, it became Brecon Cathedral in 1923.

Christ College, founded by Henry VIII in 1541 is built on the site of a 13th

*".....there are
numerous
farmhouses,
guesthouses,
inns and hotels
offering bed and
breakfast in the
area ....."*

*".....the bluebell,
sadly disappearing
from many parts
of the country, can
still be seen in
huge numbers in
the Usk valley ....."*

The River Usk has a well-deserved reputation as a trout and salmon river though in recent years (in common with most rivers in Britain) the numbers of salmon have diminished. It has also been famed for the richness of its fly life though this has suffered from modern farming practices. Nevertheless it is a fine river, still supporting a good stock of fish and a wide rage of insect species.

The Salmon start to run in March. At first they are few but can be very large. They become more numerous as the spring progresses and in the early summer are joined by the Grilse, a small salmon which has spent only one year in the sea. March also heralds the first of numerous species of flies which provide food for the trout. The flies have evocative names such as the March Brown, Yellow Sally, Yellow May Dun, Spring Olive, Iron Blue and many others.

Other fish in the river are Seatrout, two species of the rare Shad and three species of that primitive boneless fish, the Lamprey. The latter have suckers in place of a mouth and fasten themselves to a host fish from which they suck their sustenance. Visitors to these parts beware. If offered a dyshe of lampreys in the local hostelry, refuse. King Henry 1st of England is said to have died of a 'surfeit of lampreys'. The Common Eel is

Water Vole

Dipper

represented in the Usk and the tiny elvers arrive in large numbers in the spring after their long journey from the breeding grounds in the Sargasso sea (near the Caribbean).

Fish and flies are not the only inhabitants of the river. The Otter is well established throughout the length of the river and was present during the very lean period some decades ago when this beautiful mammal was in danger of becoming extinct in Britain. Less popular is the North-American Mink which though only a tenth of the weight of the otter has been responsible for a great deal of damage. One of its victims is the shy water vole which is becoming a rare creature. It can still be seen on the Usk but is thought to be more common on the canal.

The river is home to many birds, the oft-hated Cormorant is present in ever larger numbers and Goosanders have began to breed on the Usk in the last two decades. Fishermen will tell you that these fish eating birds will decimate the river of trout but their numbers can also indicate the plentiful food supply and well being of the river. Two migrant birds, Common Sandpiper and Little-ringed Plover, can be found along the river banks during the summer months, the Sandpiper concealing its nest in bank side vegetation while the Plover nests

on exposed shingle, relying on its cryptically coloured eggs to avoid detection.

The catchment of the River Usk drains from base rich rocks and this river has not suffered the acidification of several mid Wales rivers and a plentiful supply of aquatic insects ensures good population of two birds. Dippers and Grey Wagtails are common on the many side streams as both prefer faster flowing waters. They are generally restricted on the main river to locations where there are ripples near bridges and weirs. The Kingfisher, in contrast, prefers slower moving water and is more often found on the main river.

Cormorant

The Buzzard is common in the wooded landscape of the valley and lucky individuals may glimpse a Red Kite wandering from its stronghold in Mid and West Wales. The wooded slopes of the valley hold good populations of three other summer migrants who fly from Africa to breed here. In the spring some woodlands ring with the songs of Wood Warbler, Pied Flycatcher and Redstart.

One of Britain's favourite flowers, the Bluebell (sadly disappearing from many parts) can still be seen in huge numbers in the Usk Valley. The scent, especially if combined with that of Cow Parsley and Hawthorn can be so strong as to be almost overpowering. The valley is a stronghold of the Primrose and the Cowslip and you may see the occasional spike of the Early Purple Orchid, especially where the fields are not too intensively managed.

The banks of the river itself harbour many flowers that have become uncommon in the countryside in general. The Balm-leaved Figwort, a relative of the Foxglove and a sombre looking plant from a distance, bears close examination. The curious tubular flowers are shades of green and brown. The Nettle-leaved Bellflower, may be seen, though it is probably an escape from gardens. The parasitic Toothwort grows on the roots of Ash and Alder trees. Dame's Violet forms patches of lilac along the steep banks. Undesirable foreigners (introduced originally as garden plants) are the Giant Hogweed (please refer to note in the Practicalities section), Japanese Knotweed and the Himalayan Balsam. The last is a tall pretty relative of the 'Busy Lizzie' but is present in sufficiently large numbers to be a pernicious weed.

The mild climate and rich soil encourages the growth of specimen native trees. Wild fruit trees such as crab apples, wild cherries and wild plum abound. The mistletoe, by no means a common plant in Britain nowadays, flourishes on several species of tree in the Usk Valley. The hillsides of the upper Usk valley have remnant sessile oak woods whereas those of the lower Usk have a greater species variety with flowering cherry most noticeable in the spring.

Fishing the Usk at Brecon

".....in the spring,
some woodlands
ring with the songs
of the Wood
Warbler, Pied
Flycatcher and
Redstart....."

*".....mountains
that descend into
valleys with farms
and villages dotted
amongst the
patchwork quilt of
small fields and
enclosures....."*

TEXT The detailed route description, introduction and background notes were jointly prepared by Mike Wagstaff and John Wilkinson both of whom gave generously of their spare time to bring this publication into being.

NATURAL HISTORY NOTES
Mike Wagstaff and Jerry Lewis.

ACCURACY Local ramblers independently checked out the whole route and their many suggestions were incorporated. Thanks to Ray Silverthorne, Judy Cox, Harry Steggles, Richard McAllister and Mike Wagstaff.

LINE DRAWINGS Helen Scourse
PHOTOGRAPHY Mike Longridge.
MAPS Mark Richards.
DESIGN Stephen Paul Dale Design

CONTACT ADDRESS:
Corporate Director Environment,
Monmouthshire County Council,
County Hall, Cwmbran. NP44 2XH
Telephone 01633 644858
Fax 01633 644800
email-uskvalleywalk@monmouthshire.gov.uk.